1000 Christmas Stickers

Designed and illustrated
by Stella Baggott

Written by Fiona Watt

Contents

D1080966

How to use this book

You can put the stickers anywhere you like in this book, but you'll find suggestions on the sticker pages of where you could put them.

On the ice

20

These stickers are on page 57.

Building snowmen

22

23

These stickers are on pages 58-59.

You could use the stickers to make your own pictures and cards.

This sticker is on page 86.

These stickers are on page 74.

You could use the stickers to decorate letters and envelopes, too.

Snowy hill

Christmas tree

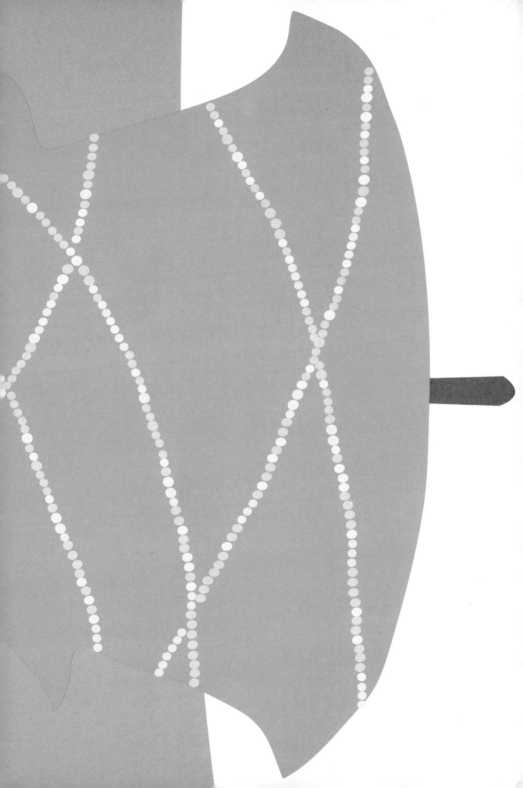

Christmas windows

Fun in the snow

Penguin party

Winter tree

Carol singing

Santa's sleigh

On the ice

Building snowmen

Christmas shopping

Dangling decorations

Snowy landscape

Santa's workshop

Skiing and snowboarding

Christmas wishes

Windows at night

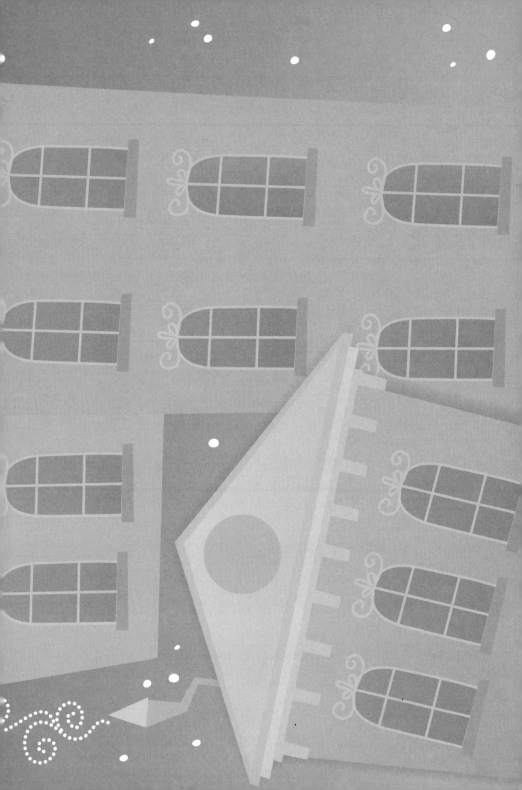

Christmas stockings

39

Street market

Festive fireplace

Snowy village

Winter campfire

Fir tree

Put these animals in any snowy scene.

Lots of Christmas tree decorations.

51

You could fill a shop window with these Christmassy stickers.

How many snowballs can you spot?

Use these stickers on snowy scenes.

53

Add these penguins to a snowy or icy scene.

Can you spot the penguin pretending to be a reindeer?

54

You could put these birds on wintery branches.

You could put these mice singing in a snowy scene.

Add these skaters to a frozen lake.

Use these stickers to build some snowmen.

Decorations to hang on ribbons.

60

Use these stickers in any snowy scene.

Spot the reindeer with the red nose.

Busy elves from Santa's workshop.

You could use these stickers on a snowy mountain scene.

Fluttering fairies to grant Christmas wishes.

You could light up the dark buildings on pages 36-37 with these windows.

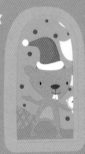

Stars and Santa for a night sky.

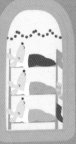

You could add these stickers to a campfire picture.

Stall holders and shoppers at a Christmas market.

Stockings you could hang on a fireplace...

... and presents and cards, too.

68

Add these shoppers to a Christmas street or market.

You could make lovely Christmas cards with these stickers.

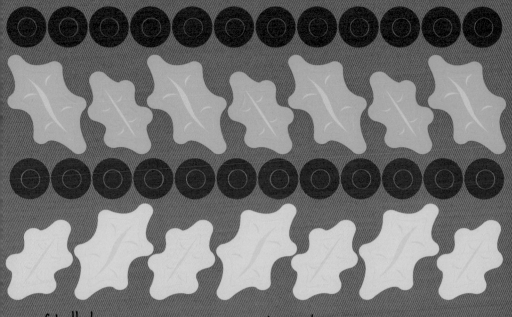

Lots of holly leaves and berries to decorate cards, presents and gift tags.

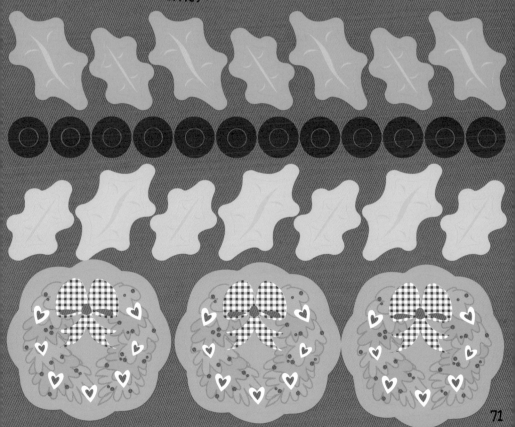

You could use these on gift tags or Christmas party invitations.

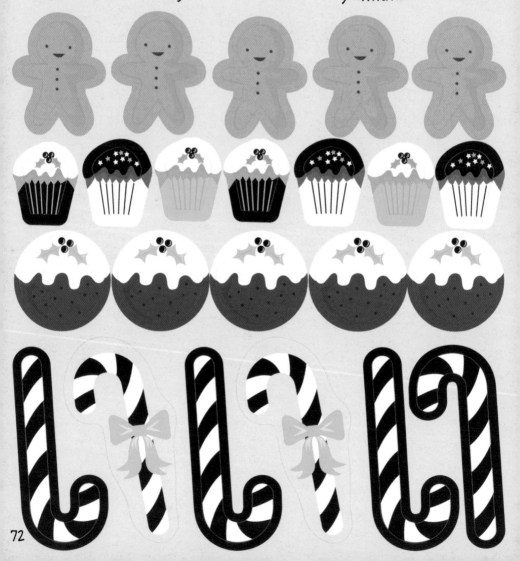

72

Stars for decorating Christmas stockings or trees.

You could put these houses in a snowy scene.

73

Can you spot the odd one out in each line?

You could put these presents under a tree or add them to Santa's sack.

You could add these festive birds to snowy trees.

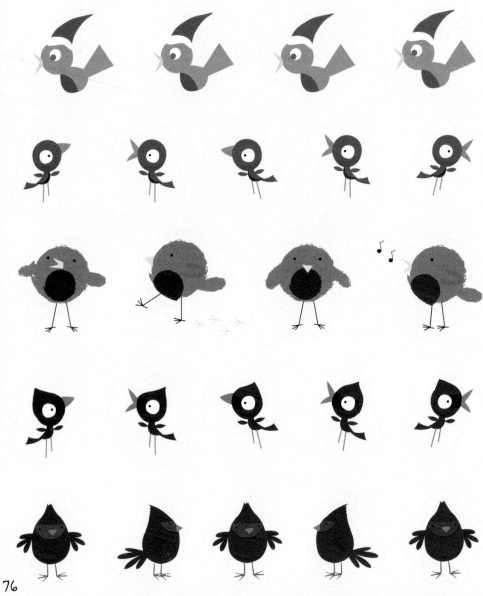

These stickers would look great on cards, tags or envelopes.

You could make Christmas cards with these snowflakes.

Lots of stickers to add to gift tags and cards.

Snow bears, bunnies and cats for cards and tags.

Can you spot the odd one out?

Lots of stockings for cards, envelopes and gift tags...

You could use these trees to decorate tags for presents.

Snowmen to add to snowy scenes.

How many blue hats can you spot?

84

Pretty trees for decorating cards.

85

Labels for cards, presents and envelopes.

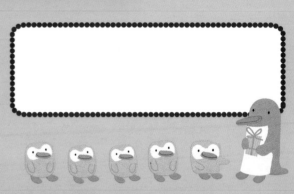

You could use these on presents and envelopes.

88

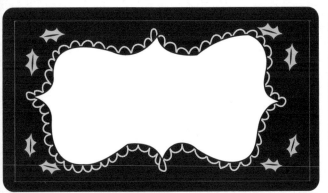
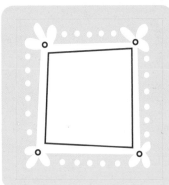